EDINBURGH CITY LIBRARIES

Please return/renew this item by the last date shown.
To renew quote your borrower number.

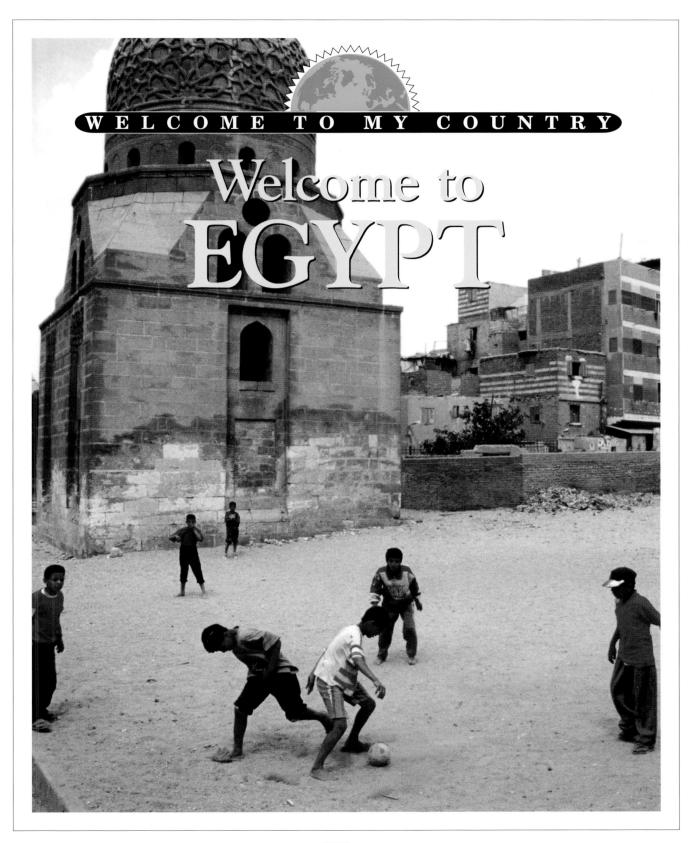

WELCOME TO MY COUNTRY

Welcome to
EGYPT

W
FRANKLIN WATTS
LONDON•SYDNEY

This edition first published in 2006 by
Franklin Watts
338 Euston Road
London NW1 3BH

This edition is published for sale only in the United Kingdom and Eire.

© Marshall Cavendish International (Asia) Pte Ltd 2006
Originated and designed by Times Editions–Marshall Cavendish
An imprint of Marshall Cavendish International (Asia) Pte Ltd
1 New Industrial Road, Singapore 536196

Written by: Nicole Frank & Susan L. Wilson
Designer: Bernard Go
Picture researchers: Thomas Khoo & Joshua Ang

A CIP catalogue record for this book
is available from the British Library.

ISBN-10: 0 7496 7016 9
ISBN-13: 978 0 7496 7016 0

Printed in Malaysia

Franklin Watts is a division of Hachette Children's Books.

PICTURE CREDITS
AFP: 18
alt.TYPE/Reuters: 5, 16, 19 (top), 45
Kristie Burns: 24, 25, 27, 33 (both), 34,
 38, 39
Bruce Coleman Collection: 3 (top), 9, 14
Focus Team Photo Agency: 7, 8 (bottom), 43
Itamar Grinberg: 4
Haga Library: 22, 23
The Hutchison Library: 19 (bottom)
The Image Bank: 18, 28
International Photobank: 30
Jason Lauré: 12
Lonely Planet Images: 1, 17
Photolibrary.com: 19 (bottom), 26, 41
Still Pictures: 3 (centre), 20
Liba Taylor Photography: cover, 3 (bottom),
 35, 37
Tan Chung Lee: 40
Topham Picturepoint: 2, 5, 6, 10, 13,
 15 (both), 21, 29, 31, 32, 36
Travel Ink: 11
Nik Wheeler: 8 (top)

Digital Scanning by Superskill Graphics Pte Ltd

Contents

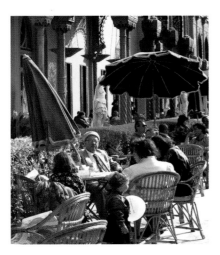

Words that appear in the glossary are printed in **bold** the first time they occur in the text.

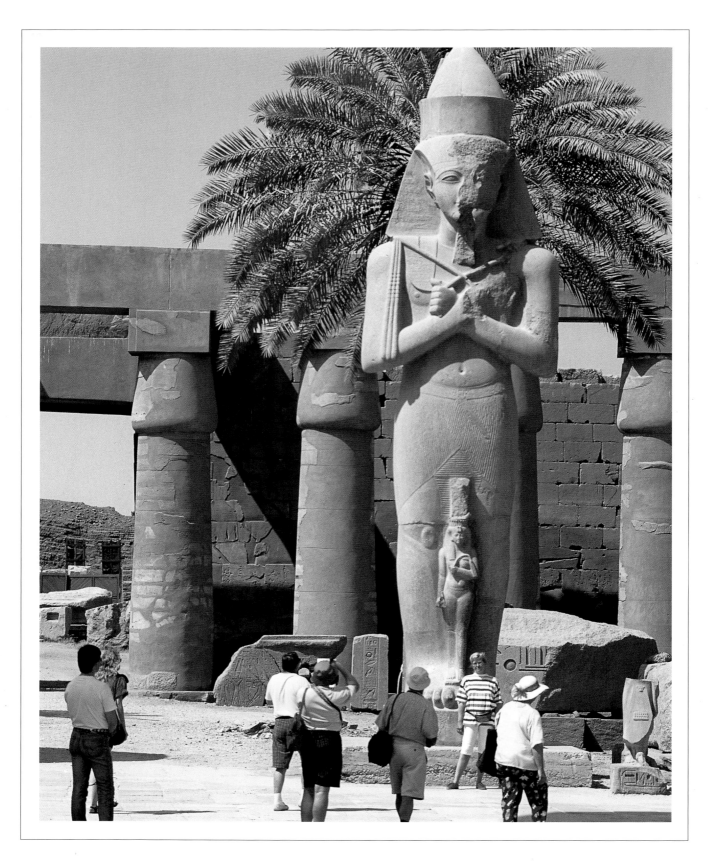

4

Welcome to Egypt!

Egypt is a land of pyramids, temples and mummies – powerful reminders of its ancient past. Present-day Egypt, however, has undergone many changes since the days of the king-gods. Let's meet the Egyptians and find out more about the "Land of the Pharaohs".

Opposite: The Temple of Karnak in Luxor was built about 4,000 years ago.

Below: The children of Egypt welcome you: *ahlan wa sahlan* (AH-lan was-AH-lan)!

The Flag of Egypt

Egypt's flag was adopted in 1952. The colour red represents **revolution**, white a bright future and black a dark past. In the centre of the flag is a golden eagle.

5

The Land

Located in the northeastern corner of Africa, Egypt covers 1,001,455 square kilometres of land. It connects Africa with Asia and Europe. The capital of Egypt is Cairo.

Most of Egypt consists of desert. The Nile River divides the country into the Eastern and Western Deserts.

Below: Egypt's Western Desert is part of the Sahara Desert, which covers much of northern Africa.

The Western Desert contains bare rocks and almost no vegetation. Mountains border the Eastern Desert along the Red Sea coast. The Sinai Peninsula of Egypt is also a desert.

Above: The Red Sea is filled with many kinds of marine life, including more than 1,000 species of fish!

The Nile River flows from central Africa and empties into the Mediterranean Sea. At 6,648 kilometres in length, it is the world's longest river. Each year, heavy rains cause the Nile to overflow its banks. Dams help to control these floods.

Seasons

Egypt has a hot season and a cool season. During the hot season from May to October, desert temperatures can reach as high as 50° to 52° Celsius. The cool winter season lasts from November to April, with temperatures of about 13° to 21° C.

Above: Date palm trees grow throughout Egypt.

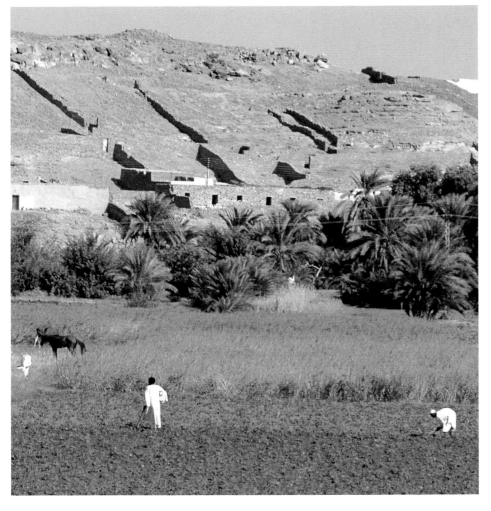

Left: Egypt receives very little rainfall. **Barren** mountains cover much of the land along the Red Sea and the Nile River.

Plants and Animals

Despite its dry climate, Egypt is home to abundant wildlife, including camels, horses, water buffalo, snakes, lizards, rats, bats and mice. Every winter, more than one million birds fly through Egypt on their journey from Europe. Egyptian law protects rare species, such as cranes and herons.

The Nile River valley, the **delta**, and the **oases** support lotus and papyrus plants. The ancient Egyptians used papyrus stems to make paper.

Left: The Egyptian cobra grows to a length of about 1.8 metres. It eats birds and toads.

History

Egypt's earliest inhabitants lived more than 250,000 years ago. In about 25,000 BCE, Egypt's climate changed, and its grassy plains became deserts. By 3400 BCE, groups of farmers were building the first settlements in Egypt.

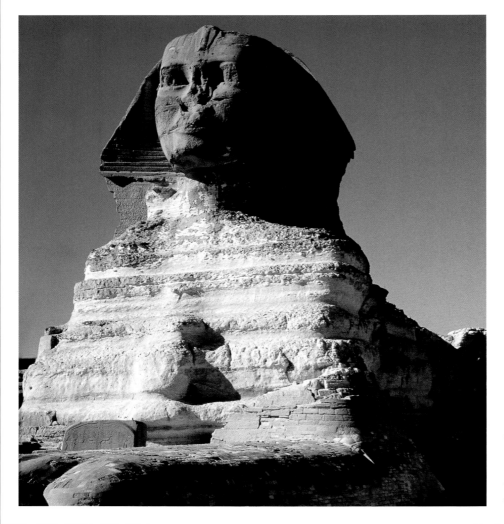

Left: The Sphinx guards the Great Pyramids. This huge monument has the face of a man and the body of a lion.

In the period 3400 to 3100 BCE, **pharaohs** (FAIR-ohs) began to rule Egypt. Pharaoh Menes (MEE-neez) united northern and southern Egypt. A succession of 30 **dynasties** ruled Egypt until Greek ruler Alexander the Great invaded in 330 BCE. About 600 years later, the Romans defeated Egypt's Queen Cleopatra VII, making Egypt part of the Roman Empire.

In 639 CE, the Arabs invaded Egypt, introducing the Islamic religion. In the 1500s, Egypt became part of the Turkish Ottoman Empire.

Above: The pyramid of Khufu attracts thousands of tourists every year.

Modern History

The British controlled Egypt from the late 1700s to the twentieth century. Egypt gained partial independence from Britain in 1922. Egyptian **nationalists** formed an organisation called the Wafd (WAH-fed) to fight for Egypt's full independence. This was not achieved, however, until 1952, when Egyptian leader Gamal Abdel Nasser led a successful revolution against British rule. In 1954, Nasser became president of Egypt.

Below: A parade of Egyptian troops celebrates victory in the 1973 war against Israel.

After Nasser died in 1970, Anwar al-Sadat became president. In 1978, war broke out between Israel and its Arab neighbours, and Sadat negotiated for peace. After talks held at Camp David in the United States, a peace treaty was signed in 1979. In 1981, Sadat was killed by **assassins** from secret groups that wanted to make Egypt a pure Islamic society.

Hosni Mubarak then became Egypt's president. He has continued to work for peace in the Middle East.

Above: Egyptian President Hosni Mubarak (*right*) meets with Syrian leader Farouk al Sharaa (*left*) and Saudi Arabian leader Al Faisal (*centre*) to foster good relations between their countries.

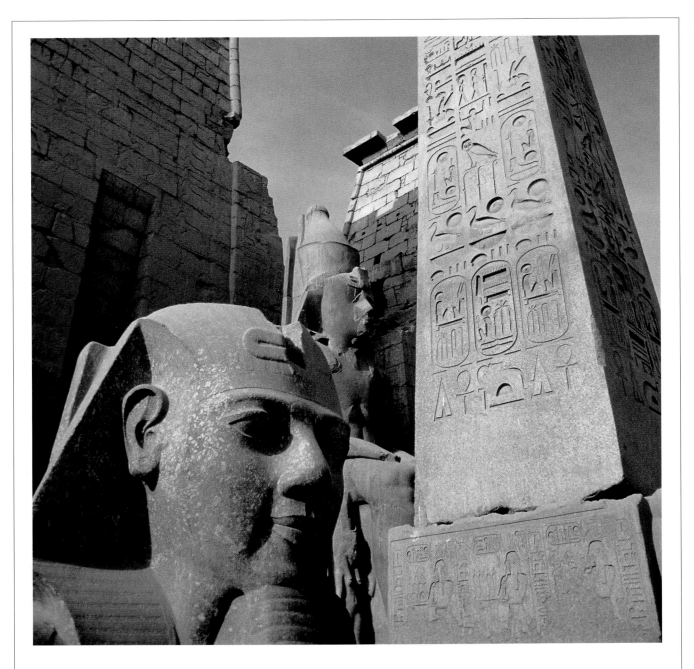

Ramses II (Nineteenth Dynasty)

Pharaoh Ramses II ruled Egypt from 1304 BCE to 1237 BCE. He competed with other rulers to build the grandest temples for the Egyptian god Amun.

Above: This giant monument, the head of Ramses II, is located in Luxor. Luxor was once known as Thebes.

Queen Hatshepsut (Eighteenth Dynasty)

Queen Hatshepsut made herself pharaoh after her husband, Pharaoh Thutmosis II, died. She ruled Egypt from about 1503 BCE to 1482 BCE.

Above: President Gamal Abdel Nasser attempted to forge an alliance of all Arab nations.

Gamal Abdel Nasser (1918–1970)

In 1952, Gamal Abdel Nasser helped launch the revolution to overthrow British rule in Egypt. Two years later, he became Egypt's president. Nasser **reformed** the new nation's economy along **socialist** lines.

Anwar al-Sadat (1918–1981)

As president, Muhammad Anwar al-Sadat helped secure peace between Egypt and Israel. He also improved relations between Egypt and the US by ending Nasser's socialist system of government.

Above: In 1978, President Anwar al-Sadat received the Nobel Peace Prize for his role in improving Egypt-Israeli relations.

Government and the Economy

Egypt is a **democratic republic** ruled by a president. Muhammad Hosni Mubarak, the current president, has been in office since 1981.

Egypt's government consists of three branches – **legislative**, **executive** and **judicial** – plus the Shura Consultative Council. The legislative branch, called the People's Assembly, makes laws and approves state policy. In 2006, the People's Assembly had 454 members.

Left: An Egyptian woman casts her vote in a ballot box in Cairo. Egypt's system of government supports many political parties.

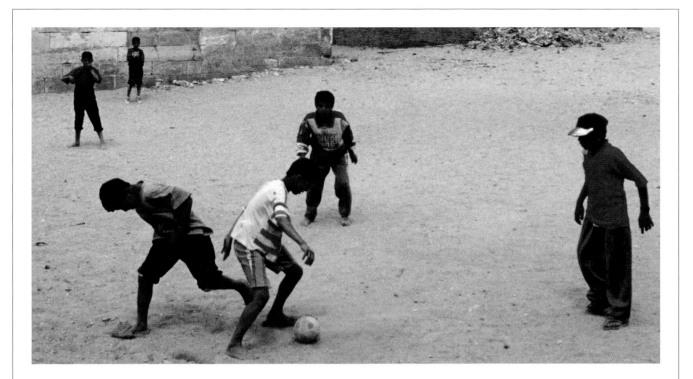

Executive power lies with the president, who is **nominated** by the People's Assembly and elected by the public. The president appoints cabinet ministers and the prime minister, who heads the government.

Judicial matters are decided by judges in a system of courts. The Shura Consultative Council advises the government but has no real authority. Of its 264 members, 88 are appointed by the president.

Economy

In 2005, the average Egyptian earned about £10,230 (15,000 euros) a year. Many Egyptians work in the service sector. About 30 per cent work on farms and 15 per cent in industry. About 10 per cent of Egyptians are unemployed. The large group of poor farmers in Egypt are called *fellahin* (FELL-ah-heen).

Left: Egypt's capital, Cairo, is a growing city, where many business meetings take place.

Cotton, petroleum and aluminium products are Egypt's biggest exports. Imported products include flour, meat, cars and steel.

Tourism plays an important role in Egypt's economy. Every year, thousands of people visit Egypt to marvel at its ancient treasures.

Below: Oil is Egypt's most valuable mineral resource.

The Suez Canal

Connecting the Mediterranean Sea with the Red Sea, the Suez Canal is one of the world's busiest shipping routes and a major source of Egypt's income.

People and Lifestyle

Although their ancestors might be **Nubian** (NOO-be-an), **Bedouin** (BED-oo-in), Arabic, Greek, Italian, Syrian or Lebanese, most modern Egyptians simply think of themselves as Egyptian.

Social class, established by birth or cultural background (not income or skin colour), determines a person's position in life.

Left: Fellahin children ride to market. More than half of all Egyptians live in rural areas.

The Nubians came from ancient Nubia in Sudan. They fished and farmed along the Nile River until the 1960s, when the Aswan High Dam was built, flooding the land.

The Bedouins do not set up permanent homes but move in search of pasture for their sheep and camel herds. However, some Bedouins have settled on the Mediterranean coast. Others are still **nomadic**.

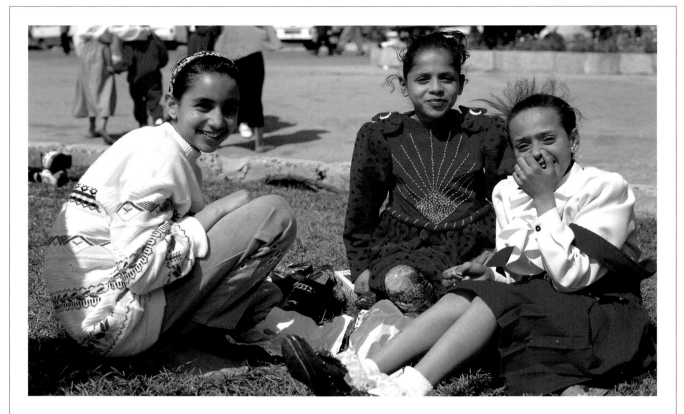

Family Life

In Egyptian families, boys and girls have different roles. Girls help their mothers at home, while boys work and play with other boys and men.

Later in life, men are seen as the source of income for their families. They are expected to have a job and earn a living. Women are responsible for taking care of the children and the household.

Above: Family outings are a fun way to spend the day. Girls and boys talk and play in separate groups.

Egyptians regard marriage and the birth of children as life's happiest events. Unlike young people in the West, Egyptian teenagers do not go out on dates. Many marriages are arranged between families. Sometimes the boy and girl know each other; sometimes they do not. Getting married involves signing the marriage contract and announcing the marriage to the public.

Below: Families visit the graves of their loved ones on *Eid el-Adha* (EYE-eed el-AD-hah), the festival of the big feast.

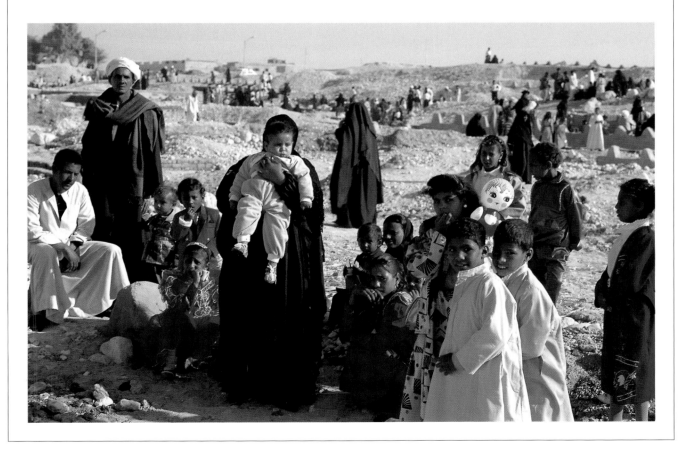

Education

Just over half of all Egyptians over the age of 15 can read and write. The Egyptian government is trying to raise this rate and prepare citizens for the challenges of the future.

Formal education for children begins at the age of six. Although primary school education is required, many poor families do not send all their children to school. Instead, they

Below: Carpet weaving is a suitable trade for girls with small, quick fingers.

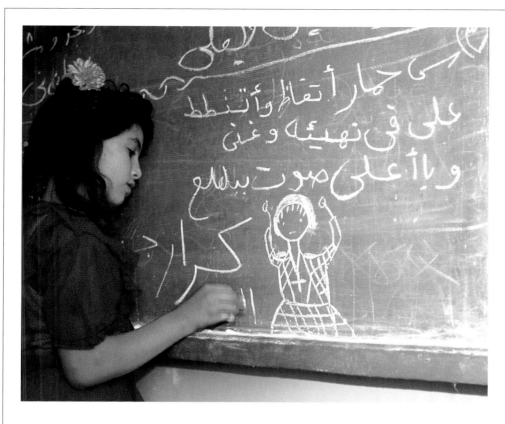

rely on the children to earn money or help out in family businesses. Three years of preparatory school follow primary school. Then, based on their exam results, students go either to a general school that prepares them for a university or to a specialised school that trains them for a technical job. University education is free for those who pass the entrance exams, but many students work instead, to earn a living.

Religion

About 90 per cent of Egyptians are Muslim. They practise Islam, the national religion of Egypt.

Islam is not just a religion but an entire way of life, combining religion with culture and moral values. Muslims worship Allah, or God. The Qur'an (KOUR-aan), or Koran, is the Muslim holy book.

Ten per cent of Egyptians are Christian. Christianity reached Egypt very early, probably during the time of the Apostles. Most Egyptian Christians belong to the Coptic Christian Church, which claims St. Mark, the author of the second Gospel, as its founder. From 312 CE until the Arabs invaded Egypt in the seventh century, Christianity was the national religion of Egypt. Today, the Coptic Christians, or Copts, are a successful community in Egypt.

Below: Egyptian children take a walk with a Christian nun. Copt schools in Egypt are open to Muslims, too.

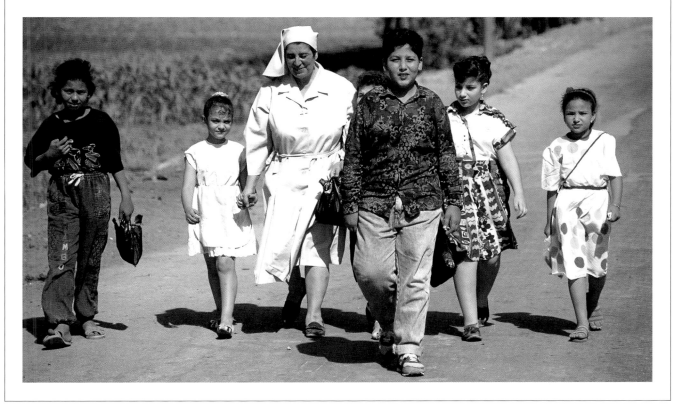

Language

Until the seventh century, Coptic was Egypt's official language. Since then, Arabic has been the national language. Today, both Copts and Muslims speak Arabic.

Arabic has many different **dialects**. Most Arabic speakers understand Egyptian **colloquial** Arabic (the informal, everyday form of the language) because Egyptian films, television and newspapers use it. The Qur'an is written in classical Arabic.

Below: Ancient Egyptians wrote in **hieroglyphics** – a kind of picture script. Hieroglyphic symbols were often carved on rocks or temple walls.

Left: Najib Mahfouz's *Cairo Trilogy – Palace Walk*, *Palace of Desire*, and *Sugar Street* – won him the Nobel Prize for Literature in 1988.

Arabic is written from right to left. Some styles of Arabic writing are truly beautiful – calligraphy is the Arabic word for "the art of handwriting".

Many Egyptian novels and plays focus on Islamic history and Western influence. Egypt's noted authors include Najib Mahfouz, Taha Husayn, Mahmud Taymur and Abbas al-Aqqad.

Arts

Egypt abounds with artistic treasures, both old and new. The ancient Egyptians expressed their religious experiences through painting, sculpture and **relief**. Ancient Egyptian art shows human figures in perfect form – young, beautiful and powerful. The artists intentionally avoided depicting old age and illness.

Left: The temple of Ramses II stands in Abu Simbel, near Aswan. Ramses II was Egypt's longest-reigning pharaoh.

Ancient Egyptian works of art tell a story. Two types of paintings and reliefs decorate the walls of temples and tombs – formal scenes and

depictions of ordinary life. Formal scenes show the world of the gods and the dead. In temples, these scenes centre around the kings and the gods. In tombs, they illustrate daily activities. In both types of scenes, the bigger the figure, the more important he or she was.

Above: The tomb of King Tutankhamun, or "King Tut", contains many beautiful and priceless objects.

Left: Unlike the pharaohs before him, Pharaoh Akhenaten and his wife, Nefertiti, worshipped only one God, named Aten. Aten is represented by the golden sphere above the figures' heads.

Sculpture and Relief

Sculpture was an early development in Egyptian art. Sculpted works featured pharaohs, queens and other members of the royal family.

The ancient Egyptians favoured two types of relief – bas-relief, where the background was cut away, and sunken relief, where figures were carved into the stone.

The Pharos Lighthouse (which is now gone) at Alexandria and the Great Pyramids at Giza rank among the Seven Wonders of the Ancient World. The pyramids are still regarded as an amazing architectural achievement.

Above: The lute has been a popular musical instrument in Egypt for thousands of years. This is the Egyptian composer, George Kazazian, playing the lute.

Left: This boy engraves a brass plate. Egyptians have always excelled at crafts and folk art, including pottery, embroidery and metal engraving.

Leisure

Most Egyptians enjoy spending time with family and friends. Many city dwellers live in the same neighbourhoods as their relatives and close friends and visit them often.

Women tend to meet in the home, but groups often gather outdoors to talk and offer each other support, as they go about their busy days.

Below: Many families celebrate holidays at the beach.

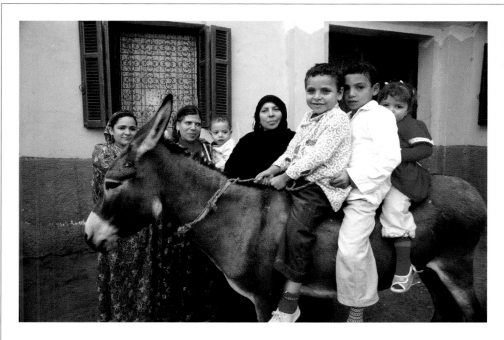

Left: Egyptian children go for a donkey ride.

Women take charge of bringing up the children and teaching them moral values, and cultural and religious traditions. Folk tales illustrate the difference between right and wrong and the importance of good friendships.

Men spend more of their leisure time in public places than women. Many men play board games at local cafés in the evening.

At night, the streets of Cairo are busy with people walking, shopping or eating at streetside stalls and cafés.

Sport

Egyptians enjoy polo, basketball, swimming, squash, volleyball and handball, but the most popular sport is football. Football fans watch the sport on television or attend games at the Cairo National Stadium or Military Academy Stadium.

Egyptian schools do not have organised sporting events. Instead, these events are sponsored by private

Below: Boys play football in front of the pyramids.

sports clubs. Most sporting events are too expensive for the average Egyptian to attend.

The two top football teams in Egypt are the al-Ahly Club and the Zamalek Club. Both are based in Cairo, and each has an impressive record of cup wins and league championships.

At the 2004 Olympic Games held in Greece, Karam Gaber won Egypt's first gold medal in 56 years in Greco-Roman wrestling.

Major Holidays and Festivals

Muslims celebrate three major festivals: *Moulid el-Nabi* (MOO-led el-NAH-bi), *Eid el-Adha* (EYE-eed el-AD-hah) and *Eid el-Fitr* (EYE-eed el-FIT-er).

Moulid el-Nabi marks the birth of the Prophet Muhammad, the founder of Islam. Homes are decorated and festivities take place in open tents. Wealthier families may go to a mosque in Cairo to celebrate the holiday, while others have a big meal at home.

Below: Sufis, an order of Muslims, connect with God through dance.

During the celebrations, merchants sell brightly coloured candy dolls that symbolise the Prophet's birthday.

Above: Schoolchildren practise for a musical they will perform during Ramadan.

Eid el-Adha (the big feast) takes place after the annual **pilgrimage** to Mecca, the Islamic holy place in Saudi Arabia.

Eid el-Fitr (the little feast) celebrates the end of Ramadan (RA-ma-DAAN), the ninth month of the Islamic calendar. During Ramadan, Muslims fast throughout the day, breaking their fast only at sunset.

Food

Except for a few distinctly Egyptian dishes, most food in Egypt is a mix of Turkish, Greek, Palestinian, Lebanese and Syrian **cuisine**.

Basic Foods and Main Meals

Bread, *foul* (FOOL) and *ta'miya* (ta-MEE-ya) are the basic foods in an Egyptian diet. Like pita bread, Egyptian bread is flat. Foul is boiled

Below: This woman is baking flat, pita-like bread. You can make a pocket in the bread and fill it with all kinds of tasty ingredients.

fava beans. Ta'miya, also called *felafel* (fey-LAH-fel), are fried balls of chickpeas and wheat.

Lunch is the main meal of the day, while dinner is smaller and simpler. Desserts consist of puddings and sweet cakes.

All Egyptians, even poor families, welcome their guests with generous meals. To be considered a good guest in Egypt, you must eat a lot!

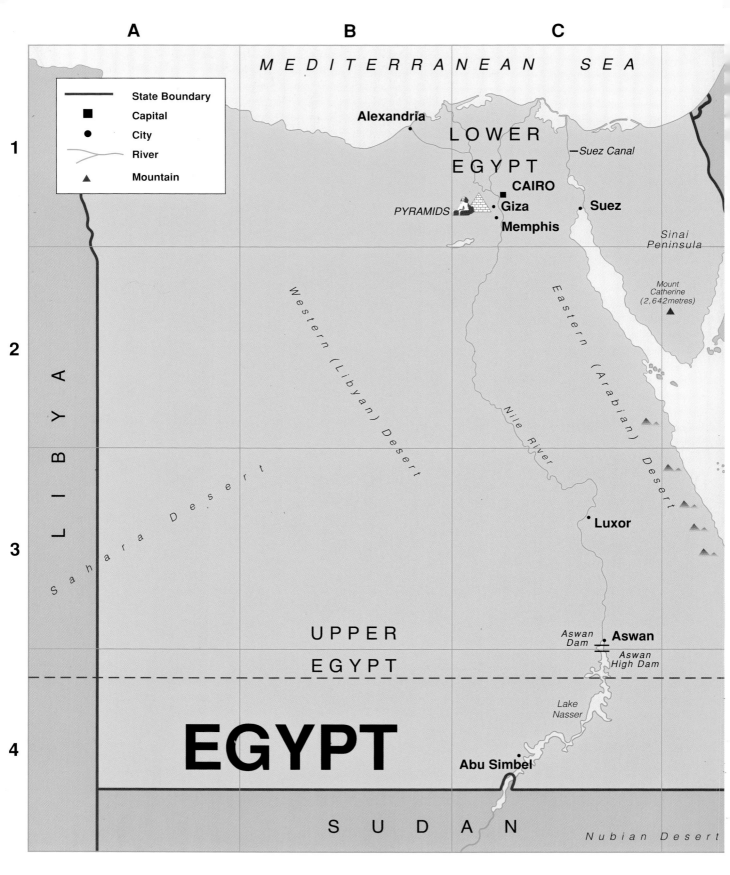

MEDITERRANEAN SEA

A **B** **C**

State Boundary
Capital
City
River
Mountain

Alexandria

L O W E R
E G Y P T

—*Suez Canal*

CAIRO

PYRAMIDS •**Giza**
•**Suez**

•**Memphis**

Sinai Peninsula

Mount Catherine (2,642 metres) ▲

Western (Libyan) Desert

Eastern (Arabian) Desert

Sahara Desert

Nile River

•**Luxor**

1

2

3

4

U P P E R
E G Y P T

Aswan Dam •**Aswan**

Aswan High Dam

Lake Nasser

EGYPT

Abu Simbel

S U D A N

Nubian Desert

42

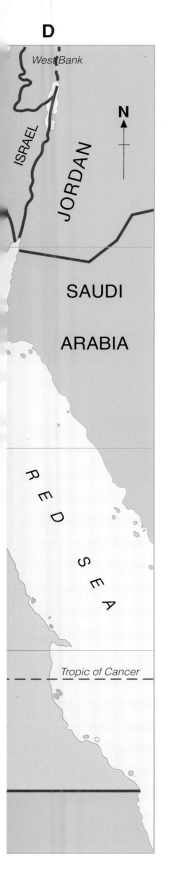

D

West Bank

ISRAEL

JORDAN

N

SAUDI

ARABIA

R E D   S E A

Tropic of Cancer

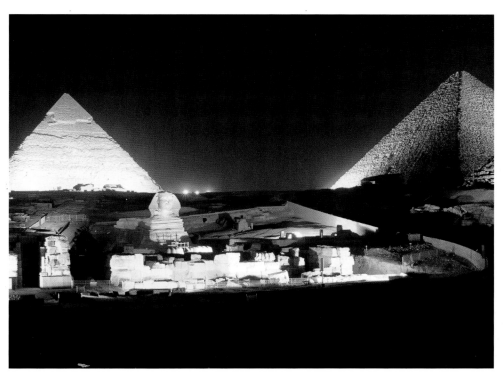

Above: As part of the sound and light show at Giza, the Sphinx tells the story of the Great Pyramids.

Abu Simbel C4
Alexandria B1
Aswan C3
Aswan Dam C3
Aswan High Dam C3

Cairo C1

Eastern Desert C2

Giza C1

Israel D1

Jordan D1

Libya A1–A4
Lower Egypt B1–B2
Luxor C3

Mediterranean Sea
  B1–C1
Memphis C1
Mount Catherine D2

Nasser, Lake C4
Nile River C2–C3
Nubian Desert
  C4–D4

Pyramids C1

Red Sea D3

Sahara Desert A3
Saudi Arabia D2

Sinai Peninsula
  C1–D1
Sudan B4
Suez C1
Suez Canal C1

Upper Egypt B3–B4

West Bank D1
Western Desert B2

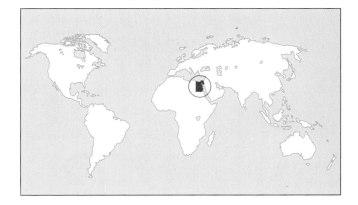

Quick Facts

Official Name	Arab Republic of Egypt; Jumhuriyah Misr al-Arabiyah
Capital	Cairo
Official Language	Arabic
Population	78,887,007 (July 2006 estimate)
Land Area	1,001,455 square kilometres
Divisions	26 governorates
Highest Point	Mount Catherine (Jabal Katrina): (2,642 metres)
Major River	Nile
Main Religion	Islam
Flag	Three equal horizontal bands of red (top), white (centre) and black (bottom), with the national emblem, an eagle, centred in the white band
Government	Republic
Head of State	President (Muhammad Hosni Mubarak, elected in 1981)
National Holiday	Anniversary of the Revolution, 23 July
Currency	Egyptian pound (7.4 EGP = 1 Euro in May 2006)

Opposite: Two Egyptian girls chat at a bazaar selling colourful Ramadan lanterns.

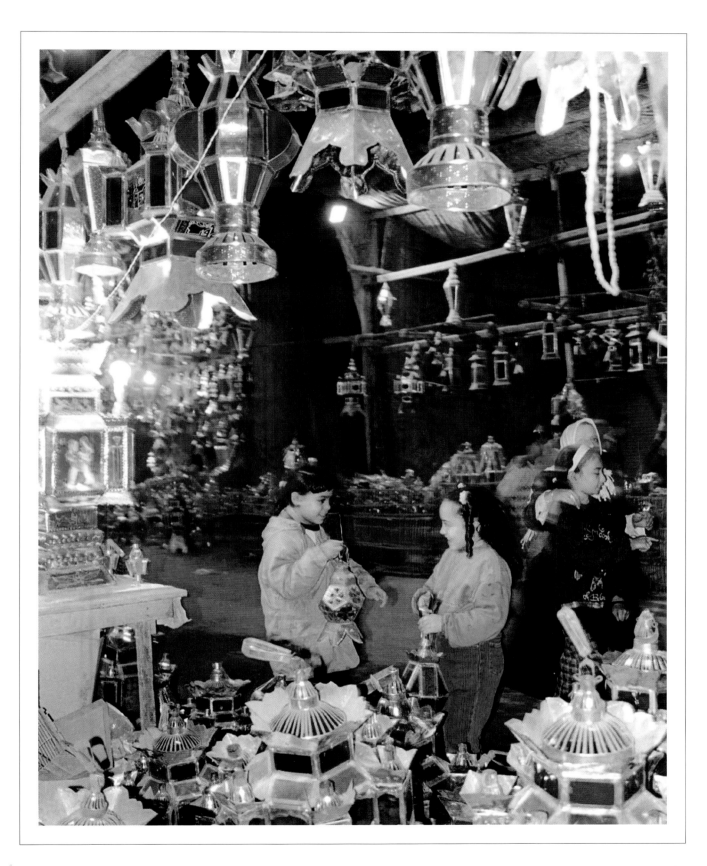

Glossary

assassins: people who murder a politically important person.

barren: infertile; not capable of supporting vegetation.

Bedouin (BED-oo-in)**:** a nomadic Arab living in Egypt, North Africa or the Arabian Peninsula.

colloquial: informal, ordinary.

cuisine: food.

delta: a flat plain at a river's mouth.

democratic: relating to a system of government in which supreme power rests with the people.

dialects: regional varieties of a certain language.

dynasties: families of rulers.

executive: relating to the administrative or governing authority.

fellahin (FELL-ah-heen)**:** the poor class in Egypt.

hieroglyphics: a picture script used by ancient Egyptians.

judicial: relating to the enforcing of justice by courts of law.

legislative: relating to the law and the making of laws.

nationalists: people who are devoted and loyal to their country.

nomadic: relating to people who do not set up permanent homes but move from place to place in search of pasture for their cattle.

nominated: proposed for an appointment or position.

Nubian (NOO-be-an)**:** a dark-skinned Egyptian from the southern part of the country.

oases: fertile areas in a desert region, usually having a spring or some other source of water.

pharaohs: Egyptian kings.

pilgrimage: a religious journey.

reformed: changed.

relief: a form of sculpture in which figures are carved to project, or stand out, from the background.

republic: a nation in which supreme power rests with the people, who elect their representatives to govern.

revolution: the overthrow of the government that is in power.

socialist: a system of government in which the state owns all businesses.

More Books To Read

Ancient Egypt: Eyewitness series. George Hart (Dorling Kindersley)

I Wonder Why Pyramids Were Built and Other Questions About Ancient Egypt. Philip Steele (Kingfisher Books)

Facts About Ancient Egypt. Jen Green (Hodder Wayland)

Wonders of Egypt: a Course in Egyptology. Dugald Steer (Templar Publishing)

We're from Egypt. Young Explorer series. Vic Parker (Heinemann Library)

A River Journey: The Nile. Rob Bowden (Hodder Wayland)

Story of the Nile. Dr Anne Millard and Steve Noon (Dorling Kindersley)

Egypt. Changing Face of series. Ron Ragsdale (Hodder Wayland)

Egypt. Letters from Around the World series. David Cummings (Cherrytree Books)

Egypt. Countries of the World series. John Pallister (Evans Brothers)

The Orchard Book of Stories from Ancient Egypt. Robert Swindells and Stephen Lambert (Orchard Books)

Websites

www.touregypt.net/wildegypt

www.ancientegypt.co.uk

www.woodlands-junior.kent.sch.uk/Homework/rivers/nile.htm

Due to the dynamic nature of the Internet, some websites stay current longer than others. To find additional websites, use a reliable search engine with one or more of the following keywords to help you locate information on Egypt. Keywords: *Bedouins, Cairo, Egyptians, Nubians, pyramids, Ramses II, Sphinx, Suez Canal.*

Note to parents and teachers

Every effort has been made by the Publishers to ensure that these websites are suitable for children, that they are of the highest educational value, and that they contain no inappropriate or offensive material. However, because of the nature of the Internet, it is impossible to guarantee that the contents of these sites will not be altered. We strongly advise that Internet access is supervised by a responsible adult.

Index